Tax Breaks *They* Don't Want You To Know About

By

Carolyn Carter

Dedications

This book is dedicated to my wonderful mother Ethel, a Guatemalan immigrant who came to the United States of America in the early 1960's with nothing but the clothes on her back, nine children and a dream. Ethel worked diligently as a nurse to raise nine children on her own. After many years of hard work, Ethel became a successful real estate investor. To my mother without you my life would be nothing.

To my son Arthur - who means the world to me and whom I love with all of my heart.

To the very special Terry - without you my days would not be filled with such happiness. I love you.

To my wonderful sister Vilma - you are like my second mother and I will never forget all you've done for me. Thanks for always being there for me big sis'- I Love you.

I also want to thank Alfred, Jean, Louise, Telford, Gertrude, Michael, and my long lost brother Carlmon (Junie) – who I haven't seen or heard from in over twenty years.

Why This Book is For You?

This book is for you if you are sick and tired of reading tax books which contain complicated IRS tax codes, convoluted mathematical formulas, equations, accounting jargon and unnecessary income tax bullshit, all of which is extremely difficult to comprehend. As a taxpayer, you need straightforward information regarding tax breaks, which you can apply to *your real-life tax situation*. Yes, there are many tax books currently on the market today, but the majority are difficult to read and most do not contain clear-cut, concise tax breaks which taxpayers can apply to their real life income tax and financial situations.

This book is written in clear and easy to understand language and highlights very *specific hidden tax breaks* that can and will save taxpayers hundreds or even thousands of dollars in taxes every year.

Taxpayers work diligently all year long and when tax season rolls around taxpayers merely want to know how they can save money on their income taxes. Plain and simple! Taxpayers don't have time to decipher complex mathematical formulas and equations nor do they have time to interpret IRS tax codes. Taxpayers want the bottom line!

For example, taxpayers want to know what they can do this year to save money on taxes next year - thus increasing their bottom line. This book will explain how taxpayers can apply *huge tax breaks* to real life tax and financial situations.

Everyone's tax situation is different – some of you are self-employed, some of you are W-2 salaried or hourly employees, some are 1099 contracted employees, some are paid on a cash basis and many are a combination thereof – but let's face it – we all want to save big money on our taxes. If the tax breaks are there − then why not learn how to take advantage of them by applying them to real life tax and financial situations?

Aren't you tired of paying high taxes? Wouldn't you rather take a long overdue vacation, buy yourself a new car or purchase your first home? Maybe you want to buy a vacation home, invest your money, save for retirement or save for your children's college education? So, why give a big chunk of your money to Uncle Sam year after year, if you don't have to?

Uncle Sam has tax breaks hidden in his closet. These huge tax breaks have rarely been publicized, because making this information available to the general public would cost Uncle Sam billions. However, taxpayers armed with this valuable information stand to save millions of dollars, while Uncle Sam stands to lose billions. This is why every taxpayer should read this book and start taking advantage of those hidden tax breaks today!

Whether you earn as little as $25,000 annually or as much as $150,000 annually wouldn't you like to learn how to avoid paying high taxes to Uncle Sam? Taxes Are Paid and Then You Die − so why not learn how to keep your money rather than give it away to Uncle Sam?

Table of Contents

Chapter One
Defining You...The Taxpayer

Chapter Two
Real Estate is the Numero Uno Tax Break

Chapter Three
The Entrepreneurial Spirited Taxpayer

Chapter Four
Educate Yourself & Reap the Benefits

Chapter Five
'Til Death or Taxes Due...Us Part

Chapter Six
Do You Owe The IRS?
(You can run, but ya' can't hide)

Chapter 1

Defining You...The Taxpayer

There are many hidden tax breaks which could potentially save you – the taxpayer hundreds or maybe even thousands of dollars on your income taxes every year, but the information is not highly publicized and taxpayers simply don't know where to go to gather valuable tax information which can be applied to real life situations when filing personal or business tax returns. No one wants to make a date with Uncle Sam, in fact almost sixty-five percent (65%) of taxpayers wait until the very last minute to prepare and file their income tax returns.

Thirty-five percent (35%) of taxpayers hire certified public accounts, whom they meet with once a year to discuss their financial and tax situations. While fifty percent (50%) prepare and file their own income taxes; without any knowledge of current tax laws or prior accounting experience. The remaining fifteen percent (15%) let their fingers do the walkin' by visiting the local yellow page directory to find an income tax preparation firm (public or private, experienced or not) to prepare and file their income taxes.

I have written this book, because taxpayers should know there are hidden tax breaks available to them - everybody needs to take advantage of Uncle Sam's hidden tax breaks. The tax breaks are right under your nose, it doesn't take a rocket scientist to figure them out, but every single year hundreds of tax breaks go unnoticed. Unfortunately, Uncle Sam is reaping the benefits of taxpayer ignorance. I think it's time we stop being imperceptive taxpayers and become well-informed taxpayers.

One thing's for sure, seasons and tax laws change from year to year, but it's the taxpayer's responsibility to stay abreast of changes in state and federal tax laws. Identify which tax breaks apply to your tax and financial situation and reap the benefit of saving hundreds or even thousands of dollars.

This book is written in easy to understand language because it has been my experience over the past 15 years, many taxpayers feel apprehensive about Uncle Sam, but they simply don't understand the language in which he speaks. Uncle Sam speaks in the same language you and I speak and I am going to make it simple for you, whether you're rich or poor, single or married, living with a domestic partner, high or low wage earners, self-employed or not – we all want to save money when it comes to Uncle Sam. So, get ready for numerous surprises hidden right under your noses and don't let this year, be like the last – reap the benefits of being a knowledgeable taxpayer by reading *Tax Break They Don't Want You To Know About.*

Let's start with the thirty-five percent (35%) of taxpayers who hire certified public accountants to prepare and file their income tax returns. Taxpayers usually meet once a year with the certified public accountant. By the way, these guys or gals don't come cheap. My brother who's an electrical engineer hires a CPA every year to prepare his personal and small business income tax returns at a rate of $150.00/hour. It's wise to hire a tax accountant if you can afford to do so – because they will take time to review your personal income tax and financial situation on an annual basis. CPA's will also advise taxpayers on how they can save money on taxes from one year to the next. If they're really smart CPA's and they don't mind hurting your feelings, they'll also tell you what you're doing right and what you're doing wrong.

It's the job of your hired tax accountant to stay abreast of current state and federal tax laws and help you apply them to your individual tax situation. Many CPA firms handle personal and business income tax preparation and have very lucrative businesses because they study tax laws and hire bright CPA's to prepare their client's income tax returns, thus saving folks hundreds or even thousands of dollars. However, there are a handful of tax accountants, who don't bother keeping up with the ever-changing tax laws and they can cost taxpayers hundreds or thousands of dollars in taxes.

So, if you decide to hire a certified public tax accountant, make sure it's someone you know and trust. Maybe a friend, co-worker or family member has referred someone to you by saying, "You should call my CPA, because he or she has saved me thousands of tax dollars over the years". That's a call you may want to make – only if you can afford to make the call. However, many of us are not sitting on a pile of cash and simply are unable to afford to hire a certified public accountant, so about fifty percent (50%) of taxpayers will make an honest, but ignorant attempt to prepare his or her personal or small business income tax returns. Although, these taxpayers have no prior knowledge of state and federal tax laws - they unwillingly take the plunge and unfortunately, the plunge costs many of you thousands of dollars every year. How stupid can you be?

Well, most of you aren't stupid at all, you can't afford to hire a CPA to prepare and file your personal income tax returns, so you go to the local post office - pick up tax forms, tax pamphlets with all of the "tax mumbo jumbo" and instead of saving big money on your taxes, you usually end up breaking even (if you're lucky) or owing Uncle Sam thousands of dollars. I am not saying we shouldn't prepare our own income tax returns, but we should prepare them with knowledge. Therefore, we as self-preparing taxpayers must be prepared to either learn our state and federal tax laws or suffer dire consequences. As a self-preparer you need to know state tax laws differ from state-to-state. Depending upon the state in which you reside, you can visit your state's website and find out which state tax laws apply to your income tax situation. Remember - be the proactive taxpayer - stop being passive and ignorant.

Start doing your homework and start gathering valuable knowledge and information, which can help you save big money on your taxes every year. If you have a computer at home with Internet access, you can visit your state's website to gather all of the information required to self-prepare your state income tax returns. If you don't have a personal computer at home, then visit your local library to access the Internet to gather information applicable to your tax situation.

Federal tax laws are listed on the Internal Revenue Service website at www.irs.gov, but I have found many of my income tax clients are afraid to visit the IRS website. Everyone has his or her own reasons for being afraid of Uncle Sam. Some of us owe Uncle Sam lots of money in back taxes, while others are simply too lazy to visit the website. On the other hand, some of us are just plain fed up with Uncle Sam's gibberish. Although, I must admit - as of November 2005 the IRS has redesigned their website, making it a bit more user-friendly - or so they say. Nonetheless, the IRS website has a great deal of information, but many taxpayers simply don't know where to begin.

The IRS website allows taxpayers the opportunity to search through the entire website for current tax laws. But how do you know which tax laws apply to you? You must first examine your own personal income tax situation, by making a list of everything applicable to your unique tax situation.

For example...

Are you married?

Do you have children?

Do you rent or own a home?

Do you contribute to a 401K?

Do you contribute to a Traditional IRA or Roth IRA? Do you own a small or large business?

Do you own a home-based business?

Do you attend college?

Are you a schoolteacher or police officer?

Are you a working college student?

Are you a civil servant?

Are you in the military?

Do you have dependants other than children?

Before you get started on your income taxes, you need to take pen and paper and write down exactly what defines you - the taxpayer. Who are you? List the intricate details related to your personal income tax situation. Then take those details and expand on them. I'll show you how...

For example, my best friend Gayle is single and works full-time as a legal secretary. Gayle lives with her girlfriend Sophia, so she has a domestic partner. Her partner was unemployed most of last year, but worked briefly as a freelance writer. Gayle has no children and has never been married. What do you think Gayle's filing status should be – Single or Head of Household?

Example One – Single

Gayle may elect to file "Single" because she's self-supporting and cannot be claimed as a dependent on another person's tax return. Gayle shares living expenses (food, rent and utilities) with Sophia and Gayle has no children or other dependents.

Example Two - Head of Household

Gayle may elect to file "Head of Household" because she supports herself as well as her domestic partner. Her domestic partner didn't earn enough income to file taxes for the previous year and therefore Gayle can claim her as a dependent. However, Gayle may not be sharing the living expenses with Sophia at all. Gayle may be the primary provider in the home and cannot be claimed on another person's tax return – so Gayle would then be eligible to file "Head of Household".

Gayle can file "Head of Household" because she supports her entire household and her girlfriend currently relies on her for food, rent and additional necessities of life. Anyone can be your dependent, but they must fit the IRS's legal definition of a dependent, before you may claim them on your income taxes. Age is not a factor when determining whether someone qualifies as your dependent. You may be supporting your parents or grandparents and they also may be claimed as your legal dependents.

Dependency Exemptions

If you want to determine whether someone qualifies as your dependent, all five of the following tests must be met:

1. Member of Household or Relationship Test
2. Citizen or Resident Test
3. Joint Return Test
4. Gross Income Test
5. Support Test

Member of Household or Relationship Test

The dependent must either reside in your household for the entire year or must be related to you. Your spouse is never considered your dependent. So, your niece, nephew, grandson, grand-daughter, aunt, uncle, godchild, godmother, best friend or anyone who passes the member of household or relationship test may be listed as a dependent on your income tax return.

Citizen or Resident Test

The dependent must be a citizen of the United States or a legal resident.   Resident aliens, residents of Canada or Mexico qualify under the citizen or resident test.   So, if the taxpayer lives in the United States and has children or relatives in Mexico or Canada whom they provide support – those children or relatives may be listed as dependents on the taxpayer's income tax return.

Joint Return Test

Taxpayers are not allowed to claim a person as a dependent if he or she files a joint return. If the person you'd like to claim as your dependent files a joint return, then by law you cannot claim them as a dependent on your income tax return.

Gross Income Test

You cannot claim someone as a dependent if he or she had a gross income of $3,100 or more for the current tax year. Gross income is defined as all income in the form of goods, money, property or services that is not tax exempt. However, there are two exceptions to the gross income test – If your child is under age 19 at the end of the year, or is a full-time student under age 24 at the end of the year, the gross income test does not apply. If you have children under age 19 or full-time students whom you provide support under age 24, then you may list them on your income tax return as your dependent(s).

Support Test

In order for the taxpayer to claim someone as a dependent, the taxpayer must provide more than half of that person's total support during the year.   Special rules apply to children of divorced or separated parents, or to parents who've lived apart during the last six months of the year. The custodial parent is treated as the person who provides more than half of the child's support. However, the non-custodial parent can satisfy this test, if the custodial parent signs Form 8332 to release his or her claim to the dependent exemption.

It's important to list a valid social security number or taxpayer identification number (TIN) for all dependents listed on your income tax return. Any inaccuracies will result in a delay in processing your tax returns. Also, the IRS could reject your return if social security numbers or TIN's are listed incorrectly.

Defining You...The Taxpayer

The only way you can start saving big money on income taxes is to first define who you are and what you're made of – this is very simple and can be done in a few days. Sit down and do this right away, so you can get an idea of the topics, which apply to your real life tax situation. If you have a home-based business, then go to the search menu on the IRS website and type in "home-based business", many topics with subheadings will appear but you should locate the topics which apply only to you. I must say - if you decide to take on the task of self-preparing and filing of your tax returns, then you will have your work cut out for you. But, it can be done. However, if you're simply not a numbers-cruncher then I wouldn't recommend self-preparing of your personal and/or small business income tax returns.

So, don't procrastinate get moving now! Start today by defining who you are – what defines you (the taxpayer) and make a list.

For example:
1. I am a college student
2. I am single
3. I am a widower

4. I have two children who are ages 8 and 11

5. I have a live-in domestic partner

6. I own a small home-based business

7. I rent an apartment, house or condo

8. I have a paid babysitter (mom, sister, niece or girl/boy next door)

9. I am a senior citizen, who works part-time

10. I own my own business

11. I pay tuition for my son, daughter, spouse, boyfriend or girlfriend

12. I recently moved from LA to Chicago because my employer relocated in the downtown area

13. I live with my parents, but work full-time

14. I worked part of last year and also received unemployment benefits for the other part

15. I worked part of last year and also received disability benefits for the other part

16. I am paid on a cash basis

17. I am self-employed (1099); I have a full-time job (W-2)

18. I want to start my own business

19. I haven't filed income taxes in 5 years or more

20. I make a small amount of money and don't know if I should file taxes or not

Continue making your list until you define all of the things in your life as they relate to your financial and tax situation. Once you've done this – if you're self-preparing, you should visit your state and federal websites to search for the topics listed. This will help you to locate the many tax breaks you've been missing out on for so many years and there will be many, I'm sure. There will be numerous tax breaks you haven't taken advantage of yet – but you can sure use the extra money now - right? You know the old cliché, "Better late than never." After you've gathered all of the information necessary, which applies to your real life personal financial and tax situation you are then ready to tackle your income taxes! You'll know which questions to ask and which topics to cover...you'll be armed and dangerous!

Now, let's discuss the fifteen percent of taxpayers who simply let their fingers do the walkin'. You peruse your local yellow page directory and locate an income tax preparer in your area. We know the big names, but we won't mention them here – let's just state the facts. The facts are you don't know who these companies hire to prepare client's tax returns, because every year they offer crash courses in income tax prep to just about anyone and place these folks in their offices to prepare both state and federal income tax returns.

These folks are not people you personally know and many do not have an accounting or any type of financial background whatsoever, but with your permission, they are blindly preparing your income tax returns. They charge you fees based on the number of tax schedules required to complete your income tax returns and the number of W-2 forms filed. They also charge fees for e-filing or they may even offer to give you a refund anticipation loan (RAL), based upon the total amount of your IRS tax refund.

I am not saying you shouldn't utilize these tax prep companies, but if you choose to do so – please go in with enough knowledge about your own personal tax situation so you know what tax breaks apply to you and take advantage of those tax breaks. Stop giving Uncle Sam all of your money, when you really don't have to.

My sister Jean used to visit the local tax prep office in her Los Angeles, CA hometown every single year. They charged her about $300.00, which included state and federal tax prep fees, e-filing fees and bank fees (on her IRS income tax refund loan or RAL) and she never really knew how they arrived at their final tax figures. Jean didn't know what questions to ask or what information to divulge, so she lost about $10,000.00 every year in tax breaks. She did this for five consecutive years. Let's do the math - $10,000.00 x 5 = $50,000.00...this is how much my sister over paid in taxes to the state and federal government. She can only go back to amend her income taxes for the past three (3) years, so even if she gets her taxes amended, she will still lose $20,000.00 which can never be recouped. Is that smart? That's just plain stupid. The ignorance of not knowing which tax breaks apply to you can cost you lots of money, so why take the chance?

After owing the IRS money year in and year out - my sister Jean wised up – she came to me one day and asked me to review her personal income tax returns to find out which tax breaks may apply to her. I did so and for the past seven years, I've been retained as her tax accountant, saving her thousands of dollars annually. Guess what - Jean almost always gets an income tax refund (large or small), but what's important is she never overpays IRS, state or local taxes. She's aware of tax breaks, which apply to her personal tax situation and she knows what must be done annually (way in advance) in order to save big money on her income taxes. Jean is no longer walking into her tax situation blindly or with one eye open and neither should you.

Each taxpayer must decide which tax road is right for them. Can you afford to hire a certified public accountant? Can you afford to prepare and file your taxes yourself, because you have enough information to do them properly? Are you prepared to walk into the local tax prep company's office with good information, so they may accurately prepare and file your personal or small business income tax returns for you? The choices you make could cost or save you hundreds or even thousands of dollars, so don't make bad choices. Go in with the knowledge required to accurately prepare and file your personal or business income tax returns and you'll come out a happy taxpayer – guaranteed!

Uncle Sam changes the tax laws whenever he feels like it - but it's up to the taxpayer to keep up with the changes. Either you can save lots of money by staying abreast with changes in your state and federal tax laws or you can lose big money by sleeping your way through tax season. I have seen so many tax clients sleep their way through tax season – it's pathetic! They wait until the very last minute to gather all of the necessary tax related documents, they dread calling a tax preparer and they simply abhor Uncle Sam. This anxiety as it relates to Uncle Sam is certainly not necessary. Uncle Sam can be a bit intimidating, but once you learn how to approach him – he can become your friend. I'm not saying you'll be bosom buddies, but at least you will not be as terrified by Uncle Sam as you've been in the past. All you need is a little tax knowledge and some common sense.

At the end of this book, you will notice I have listed state tax web links for you – all you have to do is gather the necessary knowledge applicable to your personal income tax situation and apply that knowledge. Who knows – you could end up saving thousands of dollars this year alone. I also want to encourage you to visit the Internal Revenue Service website (www.irs.gov), it may seem a bit intimidating at first, but if you visit it at least once a year, you'll become increasingly familiar with federal tax laws, how they apply to you and you'll be ready when tax season approaches next year and in future years.

Don't be a "sleeper" - wake up, get off your tush and start saving big money today! You control your destiny. You can save thousands of dollars on taxes and tuck this money away in the bank for yourself and your family or you can continue to give your hard-earned money away to Uncle Sam. I have helped thousands of people all over the United States change their lives dramatically by reading this book – change your life today by applying the hidden tax breaks revealed in this book to your life. You will see your taxes decrease, while your bank accounts increase simultaneously. Your net worth will increase and the quality of life you enjoy will surely be at its best!

Chapter 2

Real Estate is the Numero Uno Tax Break

Who'd have ever thought that owning real estate would be the biggest tax break of all? My mother Ethel, is a Guatemalan immigrant who came to the United States in the early 1960's, she rented a small house for herself and five children at a monthly rate of $65.00 a month. Fifteen years later, after working as a nurse my mother was able to purchase her first home in Los Angeles, CA for $19,000.00. It was a three-bedroom house in a middle class neighborhood of South Central Los Angeles and Ethel was happy to finally become a homeowner. Ethel's real estate taxes were about $400.00 annually and she maintained ownership of the home for over twenty-five years. After about twenty years, Ethel decided she wanted to refinance the home by borrowing auxiliary capital to invest in additional real estate. The appraisal was submitted for $145,000.00 – Ethel was in total shock. She had no idea the house she'd purchased for a mere $19,000.00 had appreciated in value over the years to an astounding $145,000.00. Cha Ching! and Bling! Bling! - Ethel accumulated $126,000.00 in equity over time.

My mother was very wise when it came to her finances. She believed in making purchases only when she had the cash on-hand to pay for them. She rarely used credit cards, although many were available to her at the time. Instead, she paid cash for everything from clothing, furniture, grocery items and automobiles to her children's educational expenses. As a result, Ethel's credit rating was A+ for over 30 years, which meant she could walk into any bank or credit union and always get a loan approval.

On the advice of a certified public accountant, who was also a personal friend - Ethel used her excellent credit rating and the $126,000.00 worth of equity in her home to borrow additional capital, which she invested in real estate throughout Los Angeles, CA. After fifteen years of investing Ethel's net worth surpassed the million-dollar mark. How did she do it? She simply used her common sense, along with good tax advice.

All it takes is a little common sense and you could master the art of saving big money on taxes, while making money in the process. Let me say it again, "Real estate is the number one tax break." For example, if you purchase a home, you can itemize deductions on your income tax returns. All or some of the expenses related to the home depending on your personal income tax situation, may be deducted from your income taxes to reduce the total amount of taxes owed. But, before you purchase real estate whether it's commercial or personal property, you must first do your homework. Find areas with low crime rates and located in or near highly industrialized areas. If you have an area in mind, research the area to find out the crime statistics, the age range of the residents, median income levels, etc. – because you don't want to invest in real estate in an area declining in value over time.

My mother was very fortunate, because she purchased a home in an area that rapidly appreciated in value over time. New York, Chicago, and California are currently the top three areas in which we see the value of real estate rising steadily and rapidly. After Hurricanes Katrina and Rita, the rapid influx of people to the Houston area caused a surge in real estate prices there as well.

You must also assess your personal financial situation. Nowadays, the minimum hourly wage in order to qualify for a home loan is $10.00 per hour. Many of you are earning two, three times this much or more – so why are you not homeowners? Maybe your credit scores are low and you think it will be impossible to qualify for a home loan. Or maybe, you simply don't realize the tax saving benefits associated with being a homeowner in America today. Whatever obstacles lie between you and owning your first home – you need to overcome those obstacles quickly and start reaping the tax saving benefits of homeownership today!

Alan Greenspan is the chairman of the Federal Reserve. Greenspan, who will be replaced in January 2006 by Ben Bernanke announces increases or decreases in interest rates. He recently announced a slight increase in interest rates in December 2005. However, rates have been very low for the past several years and there has been a boom in the housing market as a result. But, you must be wondering how buying a home can help you save big money on your taxes? Well, after you purchase your first home you may feel like you've made the best investment of your life and you'd be absolutely right. Real estate investing is something I highly recommend to my tax clients. Why rent when you can own your own home and take advantage of the countless number of tax breaks that come along with being a homeowner in America?

I'll list the **_Big 5 Hidden Tax Breaks_** or what I call **_Money-savers in Real Estate Investing_** and then I'll show you how to make each one work for you.

Big 5 Hidden Tax Breaks – Real Estate Investing

1. Mortgage Interest
2. Real Estate Taxes
3. Home Based Businesses
4. Selling Your Home
5. Rental Properties

Mortgage Interest is the cost you pay to borrow money when purchasing a home. Its interest the banks charge for lending money to the borrower. This can be listed as an itemized deduction on your income tax return, which will reduce the total amount of taxes owed by the taxpayer. You will receive an annual mortgage statement from your lender during the months of January or February, which lists the total amount of mortgage interest paid during the previous year. This total amount should be listed on your income tax return.

Many of my tax clients completely forget about mortgage interest paid the previous year. They drag their feet when it comes to gathering all of the necessary documents related to preparing their taxes. They absolutely dread reviewing the paperwork and subsequently forget to add in this crucial tax savings information. For many homeowners, mortgage interest is well over $20,000 annually, for some it's just under $5,000 annually – what's most important is its tax deductible.

Real Estate Taxes are taxes you pay annually or semi-annually on your home. April and December are the months in which taxpayers submit payment of real estate taxes. This can also be listed as an itemized deduction on your income tax return. You will receive real estate property tax statements annually or semi-annually. The total amount of real estate property taxes paid for the previous year should be listed on your income tax returns. Real estate taxes must be paid or the IRS will place a **tax lien** on your home, which means the taxpayer could possibly lose the home if the real estate taxes are not paid in the time allotted. I have had a few tax clients in the past, who've run into financial difficulties and were unable to pay real estate taxes for 1-2 years. The IRS subsequently filed a tax lien with the county recorder (usually the county in which the taxpayer resides), which attaches to all rights and title of assets held by the taxpayer. Liens typically involve real property. It's important to pay real estate taxes in a timely fashion or risk losing your home. The IRS has 30 days from the time the taxes are paid to release the lien on your home.

Levies are Uncle Sam's way of getting the taxpayers immediate and undivided attention. Usually, by this point the taxpayer has ignored the IRS's attempts at collection, which include a 30-day letter Notice of Intent to Levy. A levy attaches to bank accounts or paychecks can be garnished. The IRS can also levy brokerage accounts and even IRA's. In order for a levy to be released, the taxpayer must be compliant with all tax filings.

Usually, if the taxpayer is facing financial difficulties, (i.e. job loss) they are probably unable to make the monthly mortgage payments or real estate tax payments. If you find yourself in this position, please contact your local tax collector and mortgage lien holder, to inquire about options are available to you. You may also want to contact Freddie Mac (www.freddiemac.com) to get help with possibly refinancing your mortgage, to avoid losing your home.

Home Based Businesses are more and more popular these days. If you obtain a business license in your state, you can start a home-based business. Whether you're selling candles, gift baskets, basket weaving or consulting services – you may be able to reduce the amount of taxes owed by deducting the costs associated with your home-based business.

My close friend Richard started a business in his garage years ago. Richard was a candle-maker. He loved making candles and made beautiful, scented candles at home in his garage. Richard sold the candles to friends, neighbors, co-workers, church members and relatives. Soon the demand for his candles grew beyond his ability to make them, so his business was forced into expansion. What started out as a hobby is now earning Richard over $100,000 in annual sales revenue.

Selecting a Business Structure

When you start your business, you must select a business structure. There are **five (5) types of business structures**, but the most common are sole proprietorships, s-corps and partnerships. An LLC or limited liability corporation is a somewhat new type of business structure allowed by state statue and is also becoming increasingly popular.

A **sole proprietorship** is an unincorporated business that's owned by one individual. It's the simplest and easiest form of business to establish and in most states this type of business structure doesn't even require a business license. It's a one-man or one-woman show and a large number of sole proprietorships become very lucrative businesses. However, if you decide to become a sole proprietor, you will be personally liable for all aspects of the business. Your assets become those of the business and vice-versa. You include all business expenses on your personal income tax return.

Partnerships are developed when the relationship between two or more persons join together to carry on a trade or business. Each partner contributes money, property, labor and/or skills and profits are distributed among the partners. Losses are also shared among the partners. A partnership must file an annual information return to report income, deductions, gains, losses, etc. from it's' operations. However, partnerships do not pay income taxes. Instead, it "passes through" profits or losses to the partners and each partner must include his or her share of the partnership's profits or losses on his or her personal income tax return. Partners are not employees of the company and are not required to use W-2 forms or 1099's. Instead, the partnership must furnish copies of Schedule K-1 (Form 1065) to the partners by the date the 1065 is to be filed.

Corporations usually take the same deductions as sole proprietorships, but a corporation can also take special deductions that do not apply to sole proprietorships. The profit of a corporation is taxed to the corporation when earned, and then is taxed to the shareholders when dividends are distributed. Corporate officers and shareholders have absolutely no personal liability. Shareholders cannot deduct any losses of the corporation. Shareholders usually exchange money, property or both in exchange for the corporation's capital stock. One or more persons can form corporations - they can be relatives, friends, roommates, college buddies, domestic partners – anyone can form a corporation!

S Corps help to avoid what's called "double taxation". An S Corp is exempt from federal income tax other than tax on certain capital gains and passive income. Shareholders of an S Corp must include their share of the corporation's separately stated items of income, loss and credit, and their share of non-separately stated income or loss.

LLC's – Limited Liability Corporations are popular because, just like a corporation, owners have limited personal liability for the debts and actions of the LLC. "Pass through" taxation also applies to LLC's. Owners of an LLC are called members, while owners of a corporation are called shareholders. Most states do not restrict LLC ownership, so owners can include individuals, corporations other LLC's and/or foreign entities.

Depending on how much time you have to dedicate to your business and whether you want a large or small company – it's totally up to you which business structure you select. All structures offer sensational tax savings, but the most important thing you want to keep in mind is the **amount of liability**. Do you want to be personally liable for the company or would you prefer to have limited or no liability? If you choose to be personally liable or not, please be sure to purchase liability insurance for your company. This will save you lots of money and heartache in the long run.

Business Use of Home Expense

A **Super Huge Tax Break for a Home-Based Business** is what the IRS calls the Business-Use-of-Home-Expense. If you set up a small office in one room of your home, a portion of your home would be considered "business related" and a portion of your income taxes would be reduced by the use of your home for business purposes. Whether you are self-employed or an employee, you may be able to deduct certain expenses for the part of your home you use for business. To qualify for this deduction, part of your home must be used regularly and exclusively as one of the following:

a) Regularly and exclusively as the principal place of business for your trade or business;

b) Regularly and exclusively as the place where you meet and deal with your patients, clients, or customers in the normal course of business; or

c) In connection with your trade or business, if you use a separate structure that is not attached to your home.

Under what the IRS calls the **principal-place-of-business test**, you need to figure out if your home is the principal place of your trade or business after considering where the most important activities are performed and the majority of your time is spent, in order to deduct expenses for the business-use-of-your home.

Your home office will also qualify as your principal place of business strictly for deducting expenses for its use if you meet the following requirements:

a) You use it exclusively and regularly for the administrative management activities of your trade or business; and

b) You have no other fixed location where you conduct substantial administrative or management activities of your trade or business.

So, generally speaking you cannot deduct business expenses for part of your home that's used for both personal and business purposes. For example, if you use your living room to prepare income tax returns for clients and also for personal dinner parties, you may not deduct any business-use-of-your-home expenses.

If you are an employee who utilizes his or her personal home to conduct business, then additional rules apply. Even if you meet the exclusive and regular use tests, you cannot take this deduction as an employee, unless –

a) The business use of your home is for the convenience of your employer; and

b) You don't rent any part of your home to your employer and use the rented part to perform services as an employee.

Here's a list of **deductible expenses for business-use-of-the-home expense**:

1. Real Estate Taxes
2. Deductible Mortgage Interest
3. Rent/Lease Payments
4. Casualty Losses (i.e. Hurricane Katrina & Wilma)
5. Utilities (Phone, Gas, Water, Heat)
6. Insurance (Property, Liability)
7. Depreciation (Office Furniture)
8. Security Systems
9. Maintenance and Repairs
10. Real Property Taxes

Business Percentage (example)

You have a spare room in your home you are using exclusively as a home office. Your office is 240 square feet (12 feet x 20 feet).

Your home is 1,500 square feet.

Your office is 16% (240/1,500) of the total area of your home.

The business percentage you can claim is 16%.

I highly recommend my clients start a home-based business, whether full or part-time to take advantage of this fabulous tax benefit. If you are good at painting, knitting sweaters and even stuffing envelopes – why not start a home-based business? Kill two birds with one stone - by reducing the total amount of taxes owed and increasing your personal income level. For more information on this sensational tax break, please visit the IRS website for allowable home-related deductions and you will be pleasantly surprised.

Selling Your Home

Selling Your Home can also have great tax advantages. You may be able to exclude up to $250,000 of a gain ($500,000 for married taxpayers filing jointly) from your federal income tax return. However, to be eligible for this tax break you must have owned the home for at least two (2) full years and the home must be your primary residence. You can take advantage of this tax break every two (2) years.

Why not reap the tax saving benefits now and utilize the money saved to take a much-needed vacation or buy yourself a new car or boat? Maybe you can invest the money you save in the stock market, but who wants to give it all to Uncle Sam? Nobody! The tax saving strategies listed in this chapter relate strictly to real estate ownership. You may own a home that may not be your primary residence (i.e. rental property) or you may own a commercial building (office, beauty salon, barbershop, laundromat) – all of which have tax breaks, which can be listed as itemized deductions on your federal income tax return.

Rental Properties

My mother invested wisely in real estate. After purchasing a modest 3-bedroom home in Los Angeles, CA – she purchased additional real estate property and rented many of the homes and apartments to her children. It wasn't easy being landlord and mom at the same time – but it had its benefits. My mother realized long ago, real estate was her ticket to a better and brighter future. So, she purchased what some people would call "run-down" homes and "fixer-uppers". After purchasing the homes, she'd assess renovation and remodeling expenses and locate reliable contractors who could get the work done quickly and reasonably.

She rented the property and had a fixed monthly income of over $25,000 monthly from all of her rental units. My mother still kept her day job as a nurse and never changed her lifestyle, although her bank account grew and grew over the years – she was always the same person. I remember when I was about 18 years old, I asked my mother why she drove a Buick Regal instead of a Mercedes Benz or Jaguar and her response was "I don't need a car to determine who I am – my bank account does it for me".

Wouldn't you like to see your bank account grow over time while simultaneously decreasing the income taxes owed to Uncle Sam every year? Then start today by visiting the web sites listed below – assess your personal credit and financial situations and I'm sure you'll find you do indeed qualify for a home loan. Where can taxpayers find real estate at affordable prices? Lots of folks tell you there are loads of real estate out there currently selling well below market value…but where can taxpayers locate these types of properties? Here is a list of the websites you should visit…

www.hud.gov

www.freediemac.com

www.fanniemae.com

www.realtor.com

www.ocwen.com

www.mortgagecontent.net

www.treasury.gov/auctions

Remember, to do your homework by locating areas with extremely low crime rates, which are in or near highly industrialized cities. These areas are sure to appreciate in value over time. Also assess your personal credit and financial situation to determine whether you qualify for a home loan. You may request a FREE copy of your credit report from the three (3) credit reporting bureaus: Trans Union, Equifax and Experian. You may also request your FICO score for a small fee of about $5.95. FICO scores are utilized by mortgage underwriters to determine whether you qualify for a home loan and what interest-rate you will be charged.

Average FICO scores in the United States are about 670. The higher the FICO score, the lower the interest rate and vice-versa. Even if you've recently filed for Chapter 7, 11 or 13 bankruptcies - you may still qualify for a home loan. Don't be discouraged - get started today and start reaping the enormous tax saving benefits now!

Credit Bureau websites:

www.experian.com

www.transunion.com

www.equifax.com

Chapter 3

The Entrepreneurial Spirited Tax Payer

In the previous chapter we discussed home-based businesses and how owning a home-based business could save you hundreds or thousands of dollars on your income taxes. If you have a skill or special service, which can be offered to the public ‑– for a fee, then why not start a business today? Everyone is good at something. In 2005 we recognized Ozzie Guillen's talents as a successful baseball league manager. It wasn't by accident that the Chicago White Sox won the 2005 World Series, but it was due to Ozzie's sensational skills as a league manager. Mariah Carey made a fabulous comeback this year by being nominated for the highest number of Grammy's in 2005. Everyone on this earth has special talents or skills, which are marketable. It's up to you - the taxpayer to decide if you want to market your talent or skills. If you choose to market your skills and talents by starting your own business – then hats off to you! Bill Gates started Apple Computers in his garage and where is he today? You can do it too!

In order to start your own business you may be required to obtain a business license. Business licenses usually cost about $25.00 to $200.00 annually. Contact your local Small Business Administration or local Chamber of Commerce to determine exact costs associated with starting a business in your state. You may also elect to incorporate your business and you can do so by paying a small fee to the Secretary of State in the state, which you plan to conduct or transact your business. The fee for incorporating a business can range from $79.00 - $1,000.00, this depends on the state in which you plan to conduct the business. To find out fees associated with incorporating your business, please visit your state's website.

This book is not about How to Start a Business or How to Incorporate Your Business, but it's how taxpayers can take advantage of hidden tax breaks if they should decide to start their own business. You may be an artist and you may have been painting for many years, with a basement full of beautiful paintings. Instead of selling your paintings at a garage sale, why not obtain a business license and open an art gallery in your garage? If you do so, you can start enjoying the tax benefits immediately. I am an advocate of the entrepreneurial spirit, because we all have it in us. It's extracting it, which can sometimes be the challenge.

Make a list of things you are good at and start there. The list can begin like this...

1. I am good at making gift baskets
2. I am a great cook
3. I am good at fixing PC's and installing software programs
4. I am good at tutoring my kids in math
5. I am good at knitting
6. I am a great poetry writer
7. I am good at fixing cars for my friends and family members
8. I am good at sewing
9. I have excellent editing skills
10. I have excellent translation skills

And the list goes on and on. List your skills and special talents and hone in on one you'd find great enjoyment doing in your spare time. If you like to cook, you may have always wanted to open up your own restaurant or deli. This is a dream one could realize with hard work, some determination and little common sense. Whoever thought realizing your dreams could ultimately save you big money on your income taxes?

My good friend Deb works in downtown Chicago and commutes daily on the Metra. On the train, she often runs into the same people almost daily, because they all ride the eight o'clock train consistently. One day, Deb was sitting next to a woman who was knitting beautiful scarves for her relatives during the holiday season. Deb inquired about the scarves, because they were so beautiful and so very soft. She said, "What beautiful scarves, did you make them?" And the woman responded with… "Oh, I do this every year for my relatives during the holidays. It's cheap and fun. I have ten co-workers who are interested in purchasing my scarves. They've already placed their orders and I am knitting them over the next two weeks. I'm only charging them $20.00 each." When Deb told me about the scarves, I immediately thought about how this woman could start her own business by selling those scarves not just during the holidays but all year round. I thought to myself, she's sitting on a gold mine and doesn't even realize it. She can make money and save big dough on her taxes simultaneously!

As you list your special skills and talents and we all have them – you can concentrate on something you enjoy doing and something that will also benefit others. For example, my husband Terry is a great cook and when we have dinner parties, our friends and relatives are always commenting on his culinary skills. They tell him things likes "…the food tastes magnificent" and ask him if he's interested in opening up his own restaurant. His response is usually, "No, I don't have the time to do anything like that. Besides, cooking is a hobby of mine, it's something I truly enjoy doing. I don't really consider it work." I thought to myself, someday Terry will realize opening up a restaurant can be both enjoyable and very profitable.

Everybody enjoys the Emeril Lagasse cooking show. Emeril is a great chef and so is my husband Terry. The only difference between Emeril and Terry is the fact that Emeril acted on his special talents as a chef. Emeril knows he can do it and Terry simply doesn't think he can. Maybe one day Terry will find the courage to open up his first restaurant. Right now he feels like it's something impossible for him. But, nothing in life is impossible – you have to want it badly enough. Then you just need to do it!

Entrepreneurs are reaping the benefits of saving hundreds of thousands of dollars in taxes. There are many tax breaks available to you should you decide to become a business owner. I will highlight the major tax breaks for you here and then it's up to you to take advantage of them.

Big 10 Tax Breaks for Business Owners:

1. Rents/Lease & Utility payments
2. Insurance (Life, Health, Liability)
3. Dues and Subscriptions
4. Meals and Entertainment (I don't mean strip clubs)
5. Uniforms, Mileage
6. Depreciation of Assets (Office Furniture)
7. Office Supply Costs
8. Outside Services (Contractors)
9. Internet Access Fees
10. Advertising Fees

Rents/Lease & Utility payments

Payments paid for rental of office space or payments paid to lease office space are tax-deductible expenses. Utility payments (telephone, gas, water and electric) are also tax-deductible expenses.

Insurance (Life, Health, Liability)

Insurance payments for employees (including yourself as the business owner) are tax deductible. Liability insurance will protect you against personal loss, should a client bring suit against you or your company for any reason. It's a good idea to have a liability policy in excess of $1,000,000. Sounds like a large amount, but these types of liability policies cost about $37.00/month, depending on the nature of your business.

Dues and Subscriptions

Dues and subscription for professional magazines and/or journals are also tax deductible.

Meals and Entertainment

Business related meals, travel and entertainment are also tax deductible. However, they must be business related. For example, a partner in a downtown Chicago law firm is planning to attend a trade show or convention in San Francisco, CA. The partner can deduct hotel, car rental, food, airline, and or taxi expenses related to his attendance of the convention or trade show.

Uniforms, Mileage

I have four (4) sisters and all of them are nurses. Two are CNA's (certified nursing assistants), one an RN (registered nurse) and another an LVN (licensed vocational nurse). They are all required to wear nursing uniforms while working. Therefore, they must incur the costs of purchasing nursing shoes and nursing uniforms. My sisters are also required to do a certain amount of driving while on the job (to and from client locations). Nursing uniforms, including shoes purchased are tax deductible. Miles traveled to and from work as well as miles traveled to each client location are all tax deductible. Keep track of your mileage in a notebook and save all receipts for up to three (3) years.

Depreciation of Assets (Office Furniture)

If you have a business, then chances are - you've probably purchased office equipment for your business. Computers, printers, desks, tables, chairs, file cabinets, telephones are all examples of business assets. These assets depreciate in value over time and business owners are allowed to deduct the cost of depreciable assets on their income tax returns.

Office Supply Costs

The costs associated with office supplies (paper, notebooks, pens, pencils, paperclips, clipboards, calculators, etc). All of these are considered office supplies and should be listed on your income tax returns as such. Please save all original receipts for at least three (3) years, just in case Uncle Sam decides to audit you.

Outside Services (Contractors)

Anyone who performs services for the business (in exchange for payment) who is not an actual employee of the business is considered an outside contractor. All fees charged to the business by outside contractors as they relate to running the business are tax deductible.

Internet Access Fees

Anyone running a business these days knows in order to be successful you must establish an Internet presence. Customers should be able to reach you via the World Wide Web, which undoubtedly will increase your sales. Nobody uses dial-up now days, because the service is extremely slow. DSL and cable can give you Internet access in a matter of seconds. The fees for Internet access are tax deductible.

Advertising Fees

The growth of your business relies heavily on how much advertising you can afford to do – How will your customers find you? How can potential customers learn about services or products you offer? It's crucial to advertise on the Internet as well as local newspapers. Direct mail is also a very effective advertising method. Running ads can be done in a very cost effective manner, but sometimes advertising may be somewhat pricey. But, don't worry - advertising fees are also tax deductible.

Recently in the news - a gentleman in New York, visited a strip club and ran up a tab in the hundreds of thousands. What was he thinking? He actually thought the tab could be deducted from his meals and entertainment business expense, because he was truly "entertaining business clients" at the strip club. Later it was discovered the tab wasn't actually as high as it was originally billed. But, this is something you do NOT want to do – don't take advantage of certain tax breaks and try your best to stay away from strip clubs. If you're actually on a business trip having a business lunch or dinner – save your receipt and deduct it. But, if you're meeting your family for a dinner at a fancy restaurant and you think it would be a neat idea to charge it as a business expense – don't do it. The IRS is aware of these types of abuses and they are watching closely for them.

Be honest when dealing with Uncle Sam and you will see – he will show his gratitude in exchange for your honesty. Uncle Sam has all sorts of tax breaks hidden in his closet, but it's up to you (the taxpayer) to seek those tax breaks out and apply them to your individual tax situation.

My mother was an excellent nurse and I never dreamed she'd become a successful real estate investor. She had no prior knowledge of real estate investing; she had no financial or accounting background, training or experience. But her success came about because she simply applied common sense knowledge to investing and taxes. She became a very successful businesswoman. You can apply your common sense knowledge and knowledge you've gained from this book and save thousands of dollars in taxes, while making lots of money in the process. What are you waiting for? Get movin'!

Small Business Resource Guide (CD-ROM) -You may request one FREE copy by calling the IRS at 800-829-3676 or by visiting - www.irs.gov/smallbiz

Chapter 4

Educate Yourself and Reap the Benefits

My brother's ex-girlfriend Jennifer has a live-in domestic partner named Jill, whom we call a "chronic college student". Jill is currently attending college to obtain a master's degree in education. It's as if she's been attending college most of her life. I don't remember a time when Jill was not enrolled in class. She's also working part-time, while attending college and has borrowed large amounts of money (student loans) to assist with college tuition and living expenses. But, Jill never seems to owe the IRS. She always brags about getting "...a big fat refund every year." What's Jill's secret?

The Economic Growth and Tax Relief Reconciliation Act of 2001 created a new tax deduction for college expenses. Beginning in 2002, taxpayers were allowed to deduct up to $3,000 in qualified higher education expenses. This tax deduction is only available for the next four years. The amount of the deduction is subject to certain income limits. For 2002 and 2003, taxpayers can take the maximum allowable deduction of $3,000 if their adjusted gross income in $65,000 or less. For married couples filing a joint return, the AGI limit is twice that amount, or $130,000. However, if you are married and plan to file separate returns, you are ineligible for this deduction. By investing money in your education, your spouse's education, your domestic partner's education or your children's education you can save big money on your taxes.

Whether you're a college student (full-time or part-time) or seeking a certificate in a specialized program of study – there are tax benefits you are missing out on. Uncle Sam offers several types of educational tax credits and I will list the Top Four (4) Tax Breaks for those seeking higher education:

Top 4 Hidden Tax Breaks – Higher Education

1) Higher Education Expense Deduction
2) Hope Credit
3) Lifetime Learning Credit
4) Student Loan Interest Deduction (interest paid on student loans)

Higher Education Expense Deduction

Higher education expense deduction means starting in the 2001 tax year, taxpayers are allowed to deduct college expenses up to $3,000 annually for four consecutive years. College expenses include money spent for tuition, books, supplies, laboratory fees and similar items. They also include the cost of correspondence courses, as well as any formal training and research you do as part of an educational program. Transportation and travel expenses to attend qualified educational activities may also be deducted.

I encourage many of my tax clients to enroll in continuing educational courses or pursue an associates, bachelors or masters degree at an accredited college or university. Many colleges and universities are currently offering certificate programs, bachelors, masters, and associates degrees via online studies. You may enroll in courses, take exams and communicate with your instructors via the Internet. So, even if you have a full-time job, there's no reason why you cannot seek higher education and reap the tax benefits. You may have previously acquired an associates, bachelors or master's degree – but have you reaped the tax benefits associated with obtaining the degree(s)? Remember, if you need to go back to have your income taxes amended – you may only go back three (3) years. Later in this book, we'll discuss amended tax returns in detail. However, if you've previously enrolled in courses at an accredited college or university, you may want to have your income taxes amended to reflect those tax breaks.

By educating yourself you are increasing your knowledge and your net worth simultaneously, while also saving big money on your income taxes. This is something anyone can do – however it's not something everyone may elect to do and yes, you'll be required to study if you plan on passing your courses with a grade of "C" or better to obtain your degree or certificate. But, remember you are enriching your mind and lightening the blow to your pocket book or billfold simultaneously. This is a fabulous tax credit.

About five years ago I recommended a tax client pursue a bachelor's degree, because he'd already successfully completed about sixty (60) units of undergraduate coursework towards a bachelor's degree at an accredited university. He dropped out of college to get a full-time job to support his wife and children. I advised him to take online courses towards completion of a bachelor's degree objective. By enrolling in online courses, he was able to continue working full-time, spend quality time with his family and complete his degree objective. By taking my advice he graduated two years ago with a bachelor's degree in Business Administration. He also reaped the tax saving benefits and recently received a job promotion earning him a $32,000 increase in his annual salary. This is a win-win situation...educate yourself and reap the benefits. Increase your salary, while reducing your income taxes!

Hope Credit

The Hope Credit can be claimed by the taxpayer if all three (3) of the following requirements are met:

1) You paid qualified tuition and related expenses of higher education.

2) You paid the tuition and related expenses for an eligible student.

3) The eligible student is either yourself, your spouse, or a dependent for whom you claim an exemption on your tax return.

You cannot claim the Hope Credit if any of the following are applicable:

1) Your filing status is married filing separately

2) You are listed as a dependent in the Exemptions section on another person's tax return

3) Your modified adjusted gross income is $52,000 or more ($105,000 or more if filing a joint return).

4) You or your spouse were a nonresident alien for any part of 2005 and the non-resident alien did not elect to be treated as a resident alien for tax purposes.

5) You claimed the lifetime learning credit for the same student in 2005.

All courses must be taken at an eligible educational institution, which is defined by the IRS as a college, university, vocational school or other post-secondary educational institution eligible to participate in a student aid program administered by the Department of Education. It includes all accredited, public, nonprofit, and private postsecondary institutions.

Also, to claim the Hope Credit, which is up to $1,500 per eligible student, the student must be an eligible student as defined by the IRS. An eligible student meets all of the following criteria:

1. Did not have expenses that were used to figure a Hope Credit in any two (2) earlier tax years.

2. Had not completed the first two (2) years of postsecondary education (freshman or sophomore years of college) prior to 2005.

3. Was enrolled at least half time in a program that leads to a degree, certificate, or other recognized educational credential for at least on academic period beginning in 2005.

4. Was free of any federal or state felony conviction related to possessing or distributing a controlled substance as of the end of 2005.

Lifetime Learning Credit

The Lifetime Learning Credit is a non-refundable tax credit up to $2,000 per family for all undergraduate level education. The taxpayer can claim the Lifetime Learning Credit if all three (3) of the following conditions are met:

1. You paid qualified tuition and related expenses if higher education.

2. You paid the tuition and related expenses for an eligible student.

3. The eligible student is yourself, your spouse, or a dependent for whom you claim an exemption on your tax return.

This credit is allowed for qualified tuition and related expenses paid in 2005 for an academic period beginning in 2005 or the first three (3) months of 2006.

You cannot claim the Lifetime Learning Credit if any one of the following are applicable:

1. Your filing status is married filing separately.

2. You are listed as a dependent in the exemptions section on another person's tax return.

3. Your modified adjusted gross income is $52,000 or more ($105,000 or more for joint returns).

4. You or your spouse were a non-resident alien for any part of 2005 and the non-resident alien did not elect to be treated as a resident for tax purposes.

5. You can claim the Hope credit for the same student in 2005.

Student Loan Interest Deductions

Student loan interest deductions are allowed up to $2,500 for interest paid in 2005 on a qualified student loan. The loan doesn't have to be your student loan, it could be for your spouse, son, daughter or domestic partner – you can take the deduction as long as you are the one making payments on the loan.

If finances are an issue, you may obtain student loans, grants and scholarships by completing a Student Aid Report (SAR) through FAFSA online at <u>www.fafsa.ed.gov</u>. Grants are considered gifts and do not require repayment by the student. The federal government gives grants to students in financial need. There are two main types of grants: Pell grants and SEOG grants.

Students who have not earned a bachelor's degree or professional degree are usually awarded a Pell grant. Currently the maximum Pell grant award is $4,000 annually and you may not receive a Pell grant from more than one school at a time.

To qualify for an SEOG grant, you must be an undergraduate or vocational student enrolled at least half time. Depending on the student's financial need, funds available at the school and the amount of aid the student is already receiving – SEOG grants a maximum of $4,000 per student annually.

Stafford loans are also available for those taxpayers seeking higher education. There are two types of Stafford loans: subsidized and unsubsidized.

> A subsidized loan is one in which the interest is paid by the federal government until the loan repayment period begins. Perkins loans are subsidized student loans.

> An unsubsidized loan is a loan in which the borrower is responsible for repaying both the principal and the interest.

For those taxpayers who do not wish to take advantage of this tax break, you are missing out on educating yourself or your family, while reaping the huge tax saving benefits and if you don't want to educate yourself then it's simply your loss.

Chapter 5

'Til Death or Taxes Due...Us Part

Jessica Simpson and Nick Lachey are in splitsville USA – the two have recently filed for divorce due to "irreconcilable differences". Celebrities still have not realized that beauty, money and power are surefire ingredients of a disastrous marriage. If one of the two parties involved in the marriage were unattractive, poor and thus powerless – that would be an incentive for one party to fight to hold onto the relationship. Usually the poorer, less attractive person tries desperately to hang onto the wealthier, more attractive person. But, when both parties involved are as beautiful and gorgeous as Jessica and Nick – there's absolutely no incentive to work hard on the marriage. Marriage takes a great deal of hard work and effort. However, I'm sure there are many reasons that caused the breakup of Nick and Jessica, but nowadays marriages have such a short lifespan – it makes many wonder if it's worth it to get married at all.

Now-a-days many won't even say their "I do's" unless a pre-nuptial agreement has been signed. Prenuptial agreements are contractual agreements that bride and groom enter into usually willingly, but sometimes unwillingly. I always said if I had it to do over again, I'd ask my husband to fill out a questionnaire before we even began dating. Because folks don't realize that when we get married, we are marrying not just the man or woman we see, but we are becoming "one in holy matrimony" with all of their debt – the part we don't see. My ex-husband Reggie had horrible credit when we met, but he was very honest and didn't hide the facts from me. In fact, on our first date he joked about paying for our dinner with a major credit card that would have been rejected because it was $2,500 over the current credit limit.

When I was in my early teens, I remember my mother advising me about my future husband. She said, "It's important for the man you select as your husband to have integrity, honesty and loyalty." She also said, "Short men always feel they have something to prove, because of their lack of height". I think she referred to it as "short-man syndrome", so she advised me to never date a short man. But, she never mentioned anything about looks (good or bad) or money. In fact, she forgot to warn me that I should probably run a credit, lien and background check, before I think about taking the walk down the aisle. Before many of us even say those magical words..."I do", we need to dig deeper, find out more about our potential future partners, because maybe, once we find out details regarding our partner's credit and financial situations, many of us probably wouldn't be saying, "I do", instead we'd be saying "I don't, so beat it!"

Years ago people married for love. Today love is just a four-letter word that means… "You've lost your darn mind". When I was in the early stages of dating my first husband Reggie, I remember telling my sister Gertrude that I met and fell in love with a very handsome guy. He was not rich or super smart, but he had character. He had integrity, he was honest and most importantly he was a hard working. My sister responded, "Girl, have you lost your mind? Are you crazy? All of the qualities that he appears to possess are great, but those qualities do not pay the rent. You need yourself a man with some money. Who cares what he looks like, as long as he can pay your bills."

Unfortunately, this is where society is today. We've lost the true meaning of "holy matrimony" and now we get married for ridiculous almost foolish reasons. It's important for taxpayers to keep in mind a few facts when getting married. Once you marry in certain states, everything (personal property, real property, bank accounts, and debts) is no longer "mine" or "yours", but "ours". California is one of the many states in which everything becomes "community property"....even tax debts. Yes, when you marry Joe Schmoe or Mary Contrary, you are marrying all of their tax debts too. Unless, the parties involved enter into a pre-nuptial agreement.

I guess I'm old-fashioned and truly love my husband Terry. He's simply been a wonderful husband and I have never thought about signing a prenuptial agreement with him. Terry's kindness, honesty, high morals and love for me make signing a prenuptial agreement meaningless. If you marry for true love, like Terry and I did – then your marriage will stand the test of time. Many marriages don't last because people marry for the wrong reasons. However, if you get married it's important to be aware of the options available when filing your income tax returns.

Married couples have the option of filing taxes with or without their spouses. The IRS has <u>five (5) different filing categories</u>: Single, Head of Household, Married -Filing Separate, Married - Filing Joint and Qualifying Widow(er) with dependent child. Obviously, if you are unmarried and without children or dependents – you will probably elect to file "Single". However, if you're married with dependents, sometimes it's difficult to determine which category you should select. First it's important to consider the deductions or tax credits available for each filing category.

Standard Deduction vs. Itemized Deduction

If your itemized deductions for the 2005 tax year total more than your standard deduction, you'd be a complete idiot not to itemize your deductions. The standard deduction has increased for 2005. However, the amount depends on your filing status, whether you are 65 or older or blind, and whether an exemption can be claimed for you by another taxpayer.

Standard Deductions Amounts for 2005

Head of Household	$7,300
Married - Filing Joint	$10,000
Qualifying Widower	$10,000
Married – Filing Separate	$5,000
Single	$5,000

Itemizing deductions will make it possible to claim things like medical expenses, insurance payments not covered by your employer, state income tax, property taxes, mortgage interest, casualty losses and additional tax credits that would not apply should the taxpayer elect to claim one of the standard deduction amounts listed above. It's important for taxpayers to save all receipts for itemized deductions for at least three years. Uncle Sam may decide to conduct an audit and it would really help if taxpayers maintained records of receipts related to itemized deductions. Without any written backup to show justification for itemized deductions, the IRS could drastically adjust your previously filed income tax returns and you may end up owing lots of money to Uncle Sam.

Single

Taxpayers who file "Single" are exactly that – unmarried persons. Single filers usually don't have any dependents to claim on their tax returns and unfortunately are taxed at a high rate. However, it may be cheaper to stay single than to marry someone with a huge tax debt. There's absolutely nothing wrong with filing "Single" if that's your actual status.

Head of Household

In general, taxpayers may select the "Head of Household" filing status only if, as of the end of the year, he or she were unmarried or "considered unmarried" and paid over half the cost of keeping up a home:

a) That was the main home for all the entire year of your parent whom you can claim as a dependent (your parent did not have to live with you), or

b) In which you lived for more than half the year with either of the following:

  1) Your qualifying child

  2) Any other person whom you can claim as a dependent

For example, if you are separated from your spouse and did not live with your spouse during the last six months of the year and you have custody of your children and provide total support for them in the home, then you may elect to file "Head of Household". However, if taxpayers are indeed married and filing separate tax returns, both parents cannot file "Head of Household" nor can both parents claim the same child(ren) on their tax returns.

Married – Filing Joint Return

Both you and your spouse must sign a joint return. If both signatures are not on the return, it will not be considered a joint return. Both you and your spouse are liable, jointly and individually, for the tax and any interest or penalty due on the joint return. This means that one spouse may be held liable for all of the tax due, even if all the income was earned by the other spouse. However, in some cases a spouse may be relieved from "joint liability" by simply asking for relieve from joint liability.

There are **three types** of "**relief from joint liability**":

1) **Separation of liability**, which may apply to joint filers who are divorced, widowed, legally separated, or have not lived together for the past 12 months.

2) **Innocent spouse relief**, which may apply to both husband and wife.

3) **Equitable relief**, which applies to all joint filers.

Separation of liability and innocent spouse relief only apply to items reported incorrectly on the return. However, if a spouse doesn't qualify for separation of liability or innocent spousal relief, the IRS may grant equitable relief. Form 8857 must be filed to request relief from joint liability.

Married – Filing Separate Return

Taxpayers who are married, may elect to file separate returns. This is probably the best way to go – because you can still keep your tax debts and tax refunds separate. This way, if your spouse owes the IRS for child support or past due tax liabilities, your income tax refund will not be offset to pay the debt. However, if you choose to file jointly, the IRS will take the refund amount to settle any past due tax liabilities or federal government debts (such as child support). Filing separately means that each spouse is responsible for the tax on his or her own return.

Separate returns means you will pay a higher tax rate, but sometimes paying a higher tax rate is much better than being forced to pay your spouses tax debt. Especially if the tax debt was incurred prior to the marriage and if either you or your spouse files a separate return, you can change to a joint return any time within three (3) years from the due date of the separate returns.

Qualifying Widow(er)

This is self explanatory...don't select this filing status unless your spouse is deceased.

Additional tax credits apply to taxpayers with dependents. A very popular tax credit is the **Earned Income Tax Credit (EITC).** Earned Income Tax Credit amounts for 2005 have been augmented. The actual earned income amount or maximum amount of income taxpayers may earn and still qualify for the credit has increased. Taxpayers may be able to take the credit if:

a) You have **more than one qualifying child** and your **earned income was less than $35,263** ($37,263) if married filing jointly).

b) You have **one qualifying child** and your **earned income was less than $31,030** ($33,030 if married filing jointly).

c) You **don't have any qualifying children** and your **earned income was less than $11,750** ($13,750 if married filing jointly).

Years ago I felt as if I had to have at least one qualifying child to receive this tax break. However, taxpayers don't have to have any qualifying children to receive the Earned Income Tax Credit. But, you may only take the credit for up to two (2) children. Also, the amount of your **EITC** relies heavily on your **AGI** (adjusted gross income).

Adjusted gross income is all of the money you earn or receive during the current tax year, minus adjustments to income. Taxpayers many times overstate or understate their AGI. If understated, you could end up paying a higher tax rate to the IRS and if overstated, you may be eligible for a larger refund from the IRS. It's important to accurately state your gross income on your state and federal income tax returns. Submitting inaccurate information could cost you big bucks in the long run.

AGI example:

Jim works full-time at Home Depot and earns $10.00 per hour. He also receives alimony payments from his ex-wife Jill at $200.00 monthly. Jim's adjusted gross income is

Wages Jim earned from Home Depot

+

<u>Alimony Jim received from Jill</u>

Jim's adjusted gross income

Adjusted Gross Income is defined by the IRS as taxable income from all sources including wages, salaries, tips, taxable interest, ordinary dividends, taxable refunds, credits, or offsets of state and local income taxes, alimony received, business income or loss, capital gains or losses, other gains or losses, taxable IRA distributions, taxable pensions and annuities, rental real estate, royalties, farm income or loss, unemployment compensation, taxable social security benefits, and other income minus specific deductions including educator expenses, the IRA deduction, student loan interest deduction, tuition and fees deduction, Archer MSA deduction, moving expenses, one-half of self-employment tax, self-employed health insurance deduction, self-employed SEP, SIMPLE, and qualified plans, penalty on early withdrawal of savings, and alimony paid by the taxpayer.

If taxpayers divorce, they are simply divorcing each other not their joint tax liabilities. Both parties will remain responsible for joint tax liabilities before and after the marriage has ended. This is why I advise current tax clients to think carefully before taking those wedding vows. Make sure you know exactly what you are getting into. If you are unsure, then don't get married. If you still want to "jump the broom", even though you have doubts, then please have an attorney draw up a prenuptial agreement and get it signed prior to the marriage.

Chapter 6

Do You Owe The IRS?

(You can run...but ya' can't hide)

The first question I usually ask tax clients is..."Do you owe the IRS?" Simply put, if you owe the IRS, you need to pay the IRS as soon as possible. The IRS offers several types of payment plans for taxpayers. The IRS is like a mole; it never goes away - so please, please pay. This why I advise all of my tax clients who owe the IRS – please contact the IRS immediately to find out exactly what you owe and why you owe it. If you don't know why or when the delinquent taxes were incurred, then it's your responsibility to find out. You may contact the IRS to request a copy or transcript of your taxes. Once you know what is owed and why, you can then proceed by making payment arrangements or amending your income tax returns to reduce prior year tax liabilities.

Amended Tax Returns are filed on form 1040X only in the case of an error on tax returns previously filed and processed by the IRS or state. If you overstated or understated your income in error, you are entitled to submit an amended tax return. If you missed out on certain tax credits, which you later realized you qualified for – by all means you should file an amended tax return. To claim a refund on an amended return, the 1040X must be received within three (3) years after the date you filed the original return or within two (2) years after the date you paid the tax, whichever is later. All amended returns must be filed by mail; no amended returns will be accepted electronically.

If you happen to have underpaid your income taxes, it's extremely important for you contact the IRS immediately, because the amount owed will increase over time. The IRS will add interest and late penalties to the total amount of taxes owed. For example, you may start out owing the IRS $1,000.00, but if you don't pay it for five or six years, it could possibly grow to a total debt of about $5,000.00. Depending on the interest rates and late penalties being assessed by the IRS, your small tax balance could turn into one big nightmare. So, if anyone reading this book currently owes back taxes to the IRS – please contact them immediately to avoid further interest and penalties.

In my fifteen years of preparing income tax returns for clients, I've found seventy percent of taxpayers do not wish to correspond verbally or in writing with the IRS. They'd rather have some else talk to the IRS for them. However, in order to have a third party (tax payer advocate) contact the IRS on your behalf – the IRS must receive written notification from the taxpayer. To contact your taxpayer advocate call 877-777-4778. Whether you obtain a taxpayer advocate, a tax attorney, a tax accountant or whomever – please make sure you contact the IRS immediately to resolve any unpaid tax balances.

How to resolve unpaid tax balances?

The IRS offers many ways for taxpayers to resolve balances owed, I will list the best ways to resolve these issues with the IRS, but depending on your personal income tax situation, only you can decide which one is best for you.

Offer in Compromise

An Offer in Compromise is an agreement between the IRS and the taxpayer that settles a tax liability for payment of less than the full amount owed. An Offer in Compromise is submitted on Form 656. This form was redesigned in 2004 to make it easier to read and understand. Unfortunately, the form is still very complicated to understand and taxpayers are having a difficult time completing this form and submitting it to the IRS. Form 656 must be submitted with Form 433A or 433B to help determine if the taxpayers qualifies for the fee waiver or exception. If the taxpayer qualifies for the fee waiver, then the Offer in Compromise may be submitted without the $150.00 fee.

Basically an Offer in Compromise allows the taxpayer to list his or her assets and gives the IRS an opportunity to make a determination of whether or not the outstanding debt can be settled for a lesser amount. For example, if the IRS determines the taxpayer is unable to pay the outstanding debt upon submission and review of an Offer in Compromise – the debt may be reduced. If the IRS accepts the Offer in Compromise all liens and levies (if any) are released immediate and several payment plans are offered.

IRS Payment Plans

The IRS offers three (3) different types of payment plans:

Cash – must be paid in 90 days or less. Taxpayers must pay the total balance owed in cash within 90 days of acceptance. Basically, the taxpayer can honestly tell the IRS "I can only pay 50% or 25% of the total balance due" and the IRS can accept it or deny it, based upon the information submitted on the Offer in Compromise.

Short-term deferred payment – over 90 days, but no more than 24 months. This payment plan allows the taxpayer to pay the debt over a 2- year period. If it's a large amount, then this is probably a good payment plan to request.

Deferred payment – payment terms over the remaining statutory period for collecting the tax. The remaining statutory period for collections is usually ten (10) years, so you may elect to pay the balance over a ten (10) year period.

It is very important taxpayers understand they must make payment on a regular basis. If they don't make payments on a regular basis, the IRS has the right to file a tax lien against the taxpayer. Liens give the IRS the legal claim to your property as security or payment for your tax debt. Liens may also adversely affect the taxpayers' credit rating. So, be certain all payment arrangements agreed to are kept.

IRS Installment Agreement

IRS Installment Agreement (Form 9465) – if you or your tax professional filed form 9465 requesting an installment payment plan, should the IRS accept your request the IRS will charge you a $43.00 administrative fee, plus interest on any unpaid taxes and you will be expected to pay the total balance due by January 15th of the following year. The penalty is one quarter (1/4) of one percent (1%) each month or part of a month the tax remains unpaid.

If you owe Uncle Sam it is extremely important for you to contact him immediately to structure a repayment plan. He will be kind to those who communicate with him and not so kind to those who attempt to run and hide. Remember, you can run but you can't hide from Uncle Sam.

Tax Offset – a tax offset occurs when the taxpayer owes uncollected taxes and the IRS withholds the refund and applies it to the balance owed. For example, last year I had an income tax client, by the name of Charlie - who was expecting a really big IRS refund. Charlie was ecstatic about the "large refund check" he assumed was on the way - he started planning a vacation to Hawaii with his family. He confirmed hotel and airline reservations and was expecting his refund in a few weeks. Well, after a few weeks instead of receiving a check in the mail, Charlie received a notice from the IRS notifying him of a tax offset.

Charlie owed about $2,900.00 to the IRS and his expected refund was to be $4,800.00, so the IRS withheld $2,900.00 and subsequently mailed him a check for $1,900.00. Needless to say, Charlie's vacation plans were immediately canceled.

Sometimes the taxpayer is unaware of taxes being owed to Uncle Sam. I wouldn't recommend calling the IRS to inquire as to whether a debt is owed, because you certainly don't want to give them any ideas...but you should always keep your address current with the IRS (Form 8822) and report any changes immediately. This way, if the IRS needs to contact you at any point in the future, they will have your current mailing address on file and contact you immediately. Once contacted, the taxpayer can attempt to resolve the matter without delay.

Child Support

If the taxpayer owes child support, the IRS will also offset the taxpayer's income tax refund and withhold all or a portion thereof, depending on the amount of child support owed. Many tax clients, who weren't aware of a court order to pay child support, were unhappily surprised when they waited patiently for their income tax refunds last year. The IRS will forward any unpaid child support to the District Attorney's Child Support Division who's handling the taxpayer's child support case.

Late Filers

The IRS will begin accepting e-filed returns on January 13, 2006. Please don't wait until it's too late to file your income tax returns. This year the official filing deadline is April 17th but taxpayers may request an extension (Form 4868) through August 17th. However, without an extension form filed, the IRS will consider your taxes delinquent, without exception. It's okay to file late, if you're expecting a refund. But, why wait for your money? Usually taxpayers who are expecting a refund will file early rather than late.

During 2005, approximately thirty-five percent of taxpayers waited until the last minute to prepare and submit 2004 tax returns. The IRS accepts e-filed returns for the current tax year through April 17th. Mailed returns will be accepted through mid-October. Again, it's okay to wait if you do not owe taxes and are expecting a refund, but if you feel you may owe taxes – please file your tax returns prior to the April 17th deadline.

Audits and the IRS

A friend of mine by the name of April was audited by the IRS earlier this year. April recently relocated from California to New York and during the move; she misplaced a few important receipts, which I urged her to save as backup documentation for a large number of itemized deductions claimed on a previous year's return. Here's what happened…

April received a letter from the IRS notifying her of an audit. April read the letter carefully and put it away in her desk drawer for a few weeks. After about a month, April suddenly remembers the IRS's request for **backup documents (i.e. receipts, canceled checks) regarding itemized deductions** she claimed on a prior year's return. The letter stated that April had exactly 60 days to submit the requested items or her income taxes would be adjusted by the IRS for said prior tax year.

April searched high and low, under the bed, atop the refrigerator, in kitchen cabinets and drawers for receipts that would determine whether she could keep the big fat refund she received from a prior year or whether she would have to return the money to the IRS plus interest. Unfortunately, if the taxpayer cannot furnish "written proof" to the IRS when requested, then guess what? The taxpayer is out of luck. You lose!

April recovered one or two of the requested receipts but failed to locate receipts for large medical bills totaling over $6,200.00. Unfortunately, the IRS made several adjustments to April's itemized deductions, which drastically changed her refund amount. Because April was unable to locate her receipts, she was forced to payback the money she received, plus interest to the IRS. April wound up paying back the IRS almost $4,800.00. Talk about a blow to the pocket book. As a rule, the IRS will think you lied on your income tax returns if you are not able to furnish "written proof" should there be an audit or audit demand letter. Therefore, I encourage all of my tax clients to maintain records of all receipts for at least three years. It's better to be safe than sorry.

I was told by an ex-IRS agent, who worked for the IRS for many years that audits are indeed random. The IRS doesn't single out and selectively "pick on" taxpayers for audits as a form of "taxpayer harassment", although that's what many taxpayers believe. If the taxpayer is audited, the first thought that usually comes to mind is "Why me?" The answer is generally, "You make too much money", "You inflated your itemized deductions", "You inflated your losses", or "BINGO - The IRS computer singled your tax return out because of something rather unusual".

Unfortunately, the IRS is enforcing the nation's tax laws with renewed vigor, so taxpayers can expect a higher statistical chance of being audited in the future. How much higher remains to be seen, but I advise increased caution and attention to detail with your 2005 return. The surest way to receive unwanted attention from Uncle Sam is by claiming **wildly excessive itemized deductions**. This is a "red flag" for Uncle Sam, but don't let this deter you from claiming **legitimate itemized deductions** for which you can submit written proof. Professionals such as doctors, lawyers and accountants are also targeted, because they generally run their own businesses and do their own bookkeeping. Cash businesses are easy targets for the IRS. Many people in these businesses don't declare all their income, and the IRS knows it. If, for example, your occupation is listed as a hairdresser, waiter or bartender, it may raise a "red flag". If you regularly receive cash for your work, be sure to report all the money you earn, including tips.

Despite what many folks believe, an IRS audit is generally an impartial review of your tax return to determine its accuracy. It is not an accusation of wrongdoing. But it is important to know that you, the taxpayer, generally have to substantiate the entries on your return. The IRS does not necessarily have to disprove anything. For example, if you gave $1,000 worth of old clothing to a charity but did not receive a receipt or have written proof that such a gift was made, you could be in trouble if you're audited. If the IRS questions the deduction and you cannot provide proper evidence that a gift, in such amount, was made, the deduction may be disallowed.

The IRS mandates that certain deductions must exceed a minimum percentage of your income before you can claim them. For example, medical deductions must exceed 7.5% of your income, and casualty loss deductions must exceed 10% before you can claim them. Only a small number of taxpayers satisfy these qualifications, so if you claim these deductions, keep careful records.

Charitable Contributions

The IRS is also likely to look at your contributions to charity. If you deduct more than the IRS's statistical norms, you may be audited. You must have a receipt containing certain specific information (not just a canceled check) for any single donation of $250 or more. If you do not have a receipt, the IRS may disallow the deduction.

The IRS may also audit if they receive a tip that you are cheating on your tax returns. Who might tip the IRS off? Maybe your pissed off ex-husband or ex-wife. Maybe your pissed off and very wicked ex-girlfriend or maybe someone who just doesn't like you and wants to see you miserable. Believe me an

IRS audit can make you miserable, particularly if you don't have the documentation to back up your deductions. My advise, if you don't have proof to support your deductions, don't claim them on your tax returns. You're taking a risk that could cost you lots of money in the long run and it's just not worth it.

IRS Audit Priorities

The IRS has a way of locating what I call "**high priority taxpayers**" when selecting taxpayers for audits. The IRS will look for the following characteristics and make these returns "**high audit priority**":

- Offshore credit card users
- High-risk, high-income taxpayers
- Abusive schemes and promoter investigations
- High-income non-filers
- Unreported income

Offshore credit cards

Offshore credit cards are certainly not illegal, but you can bet that if you conduct lots of business with offshore accounts, Uncle Sam will be in hot pursuit.

High-risk, high-income taxpayers

Taxpayers who earn wages in the six figure income brackets, should also be aware that Uncle Sam is watching your returns with a keen eye. If you make too much money, you need to be certain every tax break listed on your tax return can be accounted for – which means you'd better have some backup documentation to support each tax credit you claim. If not, Uncle Sam will tax you straight to the bank. Indeed, you'll have to go back to the bank to get the refund money already received and pay it back to Uncle Sam plus interest.

Abusive schemes and promoter investigations

> **Schemes**, reducing a person's tax liability by claiming inflated expenses, false deductions, unallowable credits or excessive exemptions.

> **Frivolous return arguments**, telling taxpayers compliance is voluntary or the U.S. Constitution does not provide for tax collection.

> **Promotion of slavery reparation claims** or scams that claim compensation for people who have ancestors who were slaves.

> **Abusive shelters and trusts**, investments established for the purpose of hiding income from taxation.

> **Employment tax schemes**, employee leasing, paying in cash and filing false payroll tax returns.

All of the tax schemes listed above will be prosecuted to the fullest extent by the IRS. Don't fall prey to anyone who promises to reduce your tax liability by inflating expenses, falsifying deductions, unallowable credits or taking too many exemption credits. This will be a "red flag" for the IRS and believe me, they will conduct an audit.

A group claiming they should be entitled to slave reparations were in the news recently and I don't understand how anyone could expect to be compensated on their income tax returns for anything that happened 30 or 40 years ago to their ancestors. Legally, even if your ancestors were slaves, you cannot claim credit for slave reparations on your tax returns.

I advise my tax clients to be aware of anyone promising to drastically reduce your tax liability or promising super-large refunds...if they can't do this for you legally, then watch out. The taxpayer will be liable for his or her tax return. Remember, your signature will be on the tax return, which means you've carefully reviewed the return and agree with all figures contained therein.

High-income, non-filers

The IRS has a supercomputer, which keeps track of high wage earners who never file income taxes. These folks will eventually be audited by the IRS for all "un-filed taxes" in which the taxpayer earned a substantial amount of taxable income. The IRS will prepare the tax return for these taxpayers and subsequently send them a huge tax bill plus interest and late penalties.

Unreported income

Unreported income represents the largest component of the tax gap. The IRS has developed a new tool for identifying returns with a high probability of unreported income. The new tool is known as the **Unreported Income Discriminant Index Formula** or (**UI DIF**).

All individual returns have traditionally been assigned a **DIF score** rating the probability of inaccurate information on the return. The new **UI DIF score** rates the probability of income being omitted from the return. The IRS has customarily used indirect examination methods to identify unreported income but until now has had no systemic method for selecting the returns at highest risk for unreported income. UI DIF gives the IRS the ability to systemically identify returns at high risk for unreported income and since the Fall of 2002, all returns submitted have received a UI DIF score in addition to the traditional DIF score.

You can run, but ya' cant hide...

I once met a woman who moved from one state to another to avoid paying state taxes. This is what I call "**jumpin' state**" and the only problem is when you decide to return back to the state in which the taxes are owed, you will eventually have to pay the delinquent taxes plus late penalties. I advise you to face the music and pay your past due taxes as soon as possible. Moving around from state to state, may work for those trying to **evade state taxes**, but will not work for federal tax debts. The feds will follow you from point A to point B and tack on interest, plus interest and late penalties and you'll wish you never tried to run from Uncle Sam.

The Social Security Administration (www.ssa.gov) mails out annual statements to taxpayers summarizing total wages earned and projected monthly benefits to be paid upon retirement, disability or death. Your employer in conjunction with the Social Security Administration reports wages earned to the IRS. There's no way taxpayers can get away with under-reporting wages earned, unless you are being paid in the form of cash. If you are being paid with cash, please report all wages (including tips) to the IRS. Understating or under-reporting your income will only hurt you in the end. Should the IRS discover unreported income, you will be liable for the taxable amount due on the income not previously reported to Uncle Sam, in addition to interest and late penalties. Lots of folks use the **"jumpin' state"** tactic to avoid paying taxes, but as I mentioned it may work for state taxes, but Uncle Sam will eventually catch up with you and boy will you be sorry. My advice to taxpayers is that you should stick with the **legal tax breaks described in this book**, save receipts for at least three years, maintain good record-keeping habits throughout the year and you will be a happy camper.

This chapter is short but bitter sweet and can be summed up in a few words..."If you owe the IRS you need to pay the IRS". There's no magic potion or formula, which will make your IRS debt disappear, it will only grow in magnitude, unless you take care of it. Don't waste your time or money paying high-priced attorneys large sums of money. They will promise to make your IRS debts disappear, but these high-priced attorneys will only take your money and your IRS problems will never disappear. Some attorneys may be able to negotiate a reduction in total debt, but they'd have to be a magician to make it disappear. Trust me when I say – Only you can make it go away by paying what's owed.

An old friend of mine by the name of Lou actually stopped filing taxes about 12 years ago. Notice I didn't say, "He stopped working, he just stopped filing taxes". He continues to work and leaves a trail of IRS and state tax debt behind him, but Lou moves around so much they can never catch him. I haven't spoken to Lou in over 12 years and by now; they're probably garnishing his wages. Someone who moves around from state to state as much as he does, will eventually get caught? Last I heard Lou was planning to move to Canada. Believe me when I say, if you owe - you must pay or pick up residence in another country!

I hope the **hidden tax breaks revealed in this book** have been helpful to taxpayers around the country. Now that you have this extremely valuable information, act on it – be proactive and make some positive changes in your life.

2006 Federal Tax Rate Schedules

The following tables contain tax rate schedules, so you may compute your federal estimated income tax for 2006.

Schedule X (Single)

Taxable income is over	Taxable income is under	Tax is =
$0	$7,550	10% of tax amt. Over $0
$7,550	$30,650	$755 + 15% of amt. Over $7,550
$30,650	$74,200	$4,220 + 25% of amt. Over $30,650
$74,200	$154,800	$15,107.50 + 28% of amt. Over $74,200
$154,800	$336,550	$37,675.50 + 33% of amt. Over $154,800
$336,550	No limit	$97,653 + 35% of amt. Over $336,550

Schedule Y-1 (Married Filing Jointly or Qualifying Widower)

Taxable income is over	Taxable income is under	Tax is =
$0	$15,100	10% of amt. Over $0
$15,100	$61,300	$1,510 + 15% of amt. Over $15,100
$61,300	$123,700	$8440 + 25% of amt. Over $61,300
$123,700	$188,450	$24,040 + 28% of amt. Over $123,700
$188,450	$336,550	$42,170 + 33% 0f amt. Over $188,450
$336,550	No limit	$91,043 + 35% of amt. Over $336,550

Schedule Y-2 (Married Filing Separate)

Taxable income is over	Taxable income is under	Tax is =
$0	$7,550	10% of amt. Over $0
$7,550	$30,650	$755 + 15% of amt. Over $7,550
$30,650	$61,850	$4,220 + 25% of amt. Over $30,650
$61,850	$94,225	$12,020 + 28% of amt. Over $61,850
$94,225	$168,275	$21,085 + 33% of amt. Over $94,225
$168,275	No limit	$45,521 + 35% of amt. Over $168,275

Schedule Z (Head of Household)

Taxable income is over	Taxable income is under	Tax is =
$0	$10,750	10% of the amt. Over $0
$10,750	$41,050	$1,075 + 15% of amt. Over $10,750
$41,050	$106,000	$5,620 + 25% of amt. Over $41,050
$106,000	$171,650	$21,857.50 + 28% of amt. Over $106,000
$171,650	$336,550	$40,239.50 + 33% of amt. Over $171,650
$336,550	No limit	$94,656.50 + 35% of amt. Over $336,550

IRS and State Refund Links

IRS Refund Link

https://sa.www4.irs.gov/irfof/lang/en/irfofgetstatus.jsp

State Refund Links
Alabama

http://ador.state.al.us/

Alaska

http://www.revenue.state.ak.us/

Arizona

http://www.revenue.state.az.us/refund.htm

Arkansas

http://www.state.ar.us/dfa/index.html

California

http://www.ftb.ca.gov/online/refund/index.asp

Colorado

http://www.myincometax.state.co.us/

Connecticut

http://www.ct.gov/drs/cwp/view.asp?a=1462&q=266274

Delaware

https://dorweb.revenue.state.de.us

Florida

https://taxapp2.state.fl.us/survey/txinquiry.cfm

Georgia

http://www2.state.ga.us

Hawaii

http://www.hawaii.gov/tax/tax.html

Idaho

https://www.accessidaho.org/secure/istc/refund

Illinois

http://www.revenue.state.il.us

Indiana

https://secure.in.gov/apps/dor/tax/refund/

Iowa

https://eservices.idrf.state.ia.us/taxrefund/index.jsp

Kansas

https://www.kdor.org/refundstatus/default.asp

Kentucky

http://revenue.ky.gov/refund.htm

Louisiana

https://webtax2.rev.louisiana.gov/status/refund/

Maine

https://revenue.mrs.state.me.us/refstat/

Maryland

http://individuals.marylandtaxes.com

Massachusetts

https://wf.dor.state.ma.us/mrs/Welcome.asp

Michigan

http://www.michigan.gov/treasury/

Minnesota

https://www.mndor.state.mn.us

Mississippi

http://www.mstc.state.ms.us/info/offices/indinfo.htm

Missouri

https://dors.mo.gov/tax/taxinq/welcome.jsp

Montana

http://www.discoveringmontana.com/revenue/default.asp

Nebraska

http://www.revenue.state.ne.us/refund/refundstat.html

Nevada

http://tax.state.nv.us/

New Hampshire

http://www.state.nh.us/revenue

New Jersey

http://www.state.nj.us/treasury/taxation/

New Mexico

http://www.state.nm.us/tax/

New York

http://www.tax.state.ny.us/nyshome/how_to_reach.htm

North Carolina

http://www.dor.state.nc.us/faq/refunds.html

North Dakota

http://www.state.nd.us/taxdpt

Ohio

https://www.tax.state.oh.us

Oklahoma

http://www.oktax.state.ok.us/

Oregon

http://egov.oregon.gov/DOR/PERTAX/refund.shtml

Pennsylvania

http://www.doreservices.state.pa.us/Individual

Rhode Island

http://www.tax.state.ri.us/

South Carolina

http://www.sctax.org/default.htm

South Dakota

http://www.online-taxes.com/sd/sdrefund.asp

Tennessee

http://www.state.tn.us/revenue

Texas

http://www.window.state.tx.us/m23taxes.html

Utah

http://incometax.utah.gov/

Vermont

http://www.state.vt.us/tax/individual.shtml

Virginia

https://www.individual.tax.virginia.gov

Washington

http://www.dor.wa.gov

West Virginia

https://www.state.wv.us/secure/tax/

Wisconsin

https://prd2p.it.state.wi.us/dor/faqs/inquiry.html

Wyoming

http://revenue.state.wy.us

Best Places for 2006

Best place to have your income taxes prepared

http://www.mytaxesbymail.com

Best place to invest your money

http://www.fidelity.com

Best place to rent a car

http://www.avis.com

Best place to purchase airline tickets

http://www.expedia.com

Best place to buy a new or used car

http://www.napleton.com

Best place to grocery shop online

http://www.vons.com

Best place to buy gifts for special occasions

http://www.harryanddavid.com

Best restaurants to dine in 2006

http://www.emeril.com

Best book club to join

http://www.oprah.com/books

Important tax links for taxpayers who owe the IRS...

www.irs.gov (1-800-829-1040)

www.pay1040.com (1-888-729-1040)

www.officalpayments.com (1-800-272-9829)

To check the status of your IRS refund, you may call toll-free 800-829-4477. For automated refund information, call 800-829-1954. If you have TTY/TDD equipment, please call 800-829-4059.

You may also order forms, instructions and publications by mail. Contact the Distribution Center nearest to your home and you should receive a written response within 10 business days.

Western U.S.

Western Area Distribution Center

Rancho Cordova, CA 95743-0001

Central U.S.

Central Area Distribution Center

P O Box 8903

Bloomington, IL 61702-8903

Eastern U.S.

Eastern Area Distribution Center

P O Box 85074

Richmond, VA 23261-5074